Fantastic K
Helping
Others

Elizabeth Anderson Lopez

Publishing Credits

Rachelle Cracchiolo, M.S.Ed., *Publisher*
Conni Medina, M.A.Ed., *Managing Editor*
Nika Fabienke, Ed.D., *Series Developer*
June Kikuchi, *Content Director*
John Leach, *Assistant Editor*
Kevin Pham, *Graphic Designer*

TIME For Kids and the TIME For Kids logo are registered trademarks of TIME Inc. Used under license.

Image Credits: p.5 Trinity Mirror/Mirrorpix/Alamy Stock Photo; pp.6, 8–9 Courtesy of Khloe Kares; pp.10–11, 12–13 Courtesy of Hirth's Helping Hands; pp.19, 21 Courtesy of the Braden Aboud Foundation; pp.22–23 Photo by Brianna Foster; p.25 Owen Hoffmann/Patrick McMullan via Getty Images; pp.26–27 Rancho Coastal Humane Society; all other images from iStock and/or Shutterstock.

Library of Congress Cataloging-in-Publication Data

Names: Lopez, Elizabeth Anderson, author.
Title: Fantastic kids : helping others / Elizabeth Anderson Lopez.
Description: Huntington Beach, CA : Teacher Created Materials, [2018] | Includes index.
Identifiers: LCCN 2017013462 (print) | LCCN 2017023369 (ebook) | ISBN 9781425853464 (eBook) | ISBN 9781425849726 (pbk.)
Subjects: LCSH: Voluntarism--Juvenile literature. | Humanitarianism--Juvenile literature. | Charities--Juvenile literature.
Classification: LCC HN49.V64 (ebook) | LCC HN49.V64 .L675 2018 (print) | DDC 302/.14--dc23
LC record available at https://lccn.loc.gov/2017013462

Teacher Created Materials

5301 Oceanus Drive
Huntington Beach, CA 92649-1030
http://www.tcmpub.com

ISBN 978-1-4258-4972-6

© 2018 Teacher Created Materials, Inc.

Table of Contents

Make the World Better

Have you ever had a bad day and then helped someone? It probably made you feel better. Doing something nice for others makes people feel good. And helping others can make their lives better.

You are about to meet five fantastic kids who feel good a lot. That is because they **volunteer** to make the world better. They have found special ways to help people in need. They help right in their own towns!

Food Drive

Words of Wisdom

Audrey Hepburn was a famous actress. She helped children around the world. She often said there's a reason people have two hands. One hand is to help yourself. The other hand is to help others.

Helping the Homeless

Nine-year-old Khloe Thompson is a student in California. She saw people living in the park near her school. She wondered whether she could do something to help them.

Khloe Thompson

She talked to her mother. They came up with a plan. People who are homeless often do not have **access** to showers. So Khloe created care bags for them. She filled plastic bags with soap, **deodorant**, toothpaste, a toothbrush, and other products.

Too Many Homeless

A survey found that there are about 100 million homeless people around the world. And that's not just adults. Many are 18 years old or younger.

Something Sturdier

Khloe knew that the plastic bags were not strong enough. She thought about what she could use instead. Who could help her? Khloe did not have to look far. Her grandmother sewed clothes for people. That meant that she had a lot of extra fabric. Khloe asked her grandmother to help her sew bags. Now the homeless people she helps have something strong and pretty to hold their items.

Khloe wanted to do even more. She started a **charity** called Khloe Kares that accepts items for her Kare Bags. Khloe is proof that one kid can make a big difference!

Toys All Year

There are many groups that collect toys. But they often do this only during the holidays. Toys can be **donated** anytime. Think about where you could give new or used toys.

Turning a Toy into Joy

Dylan Hirth (HUHRTH) proves that helping others can be fun. He turned one of his hobbies into a way to help sick kids. Dylan likes Rubik's Cubes®. And this 12-year-old is really good at solving them. In fact, he can do it in 37 seconds!

His hobby gave him the idea to donate cubes to kids at Mercy Children's Hospital. That is near his home in St. Louis, Missouri. At first, he saved money from doing chores to buy the cubes. He mowed lawns, babysat, and cleaned up after dogs.

Dylan Hirth

提示：
工中，请勿

Hospitals for Kids

In many ways, children's hospitals are the same as other hospitals. They have nurses, machines, and lots of fancy tools. But they only treat children. All the doctors and nurses are specially trained to treat kids.

Cubes Cure Boredom

After raising money on his own, Dylan created a charity. He called it Kubes 4 Kidz. Then, other people could donate money. One person gave $260. That bought 27 cubes! Dylan uses the money to buy the toys online.

Being in the hospital can be stressful, especially for children who are there for a long time. Kids who cannot get out of bed get bored, too. These puzzle cubes are fun to do. It is a chance to be creative. You can be creative, too. Think of things you like to do that can help others!

A Cube of Many Cubes

The original Rubik's Cube has six sides and a total of 27 mini cubes. At first it was called Magic Cube. Using it to make kids happy is pretty magical, don't you think?

Dylan packs cubes to take to Mercy Children's Hospital.

Building a Library

When you want to read, do you have a lot of books to choose from? Finding the perfect book is fun! But there are many people who cannot afford books.

Maria Clara is one of them. She lives in a village called Serrote (seh-HOH-chee) in Brazil. People in her village are poor. They are too poor to buy books. Some of them cannot read very well.

This is what **inspired** Maria. She came up with a way for people in Serrote to have access to many books. Some neighborhoods have two or three libraries. But in Maria's area, libraries did not exist.

Lots of Free Stuff

Have you ever been to your local library? You can borrow books, magazines, and even movies. And it's all free, as long as you return your items on time!

Beyond Books

Maria started a library. She was only 12 years old. It is called *Reading Friends Library*. She proves that kids can do big things. She knows that reading is important. She wanted people in her village to be better readers. People gave enough books to open the library. Now many people in her village can learn to read. Maria saw a problem and worked to solve it.

Reading the Signs

Imagine playing outside and seeing a sign that reads, "Danger: Keep Out." What might happen if you couldn't read that sign? Reading helps you explore the world safely.

DANGER KEEP OUT

Tales for Tails!

The Humane Society of Missouri has a fun program. Kids read books out loud to shelter dogs. Kids can practice reading, and dogs get attention. Talk about a win-win situation!

Best Foot Forward

"It is better to give than to receive." Have you heard this saying? Drew Frank sure has! In honor of his thirteenth birthday, Drew's family had a bar mitzvah. People usually bring gifts, but Drew did not want any. He asked for money. But he did not want it for himself. He wanted to buy shoes for people who could not afford them.

Drew received a lot of money. His gifts totaled more than $25,000! He used that money to buy 800 pairs of sneakers and socks!

What Is a Bar Mitzvah?

In the Jewish faith, boys and girls become adults around the age of 13. It is tradition to mark this big change with a religious service. It is called a bar mitzvah for boys. For girls, it is called a bat mitzvah. They put in a lot of work for the event. Afterward, there often is a big party. They celebrate their hard work.

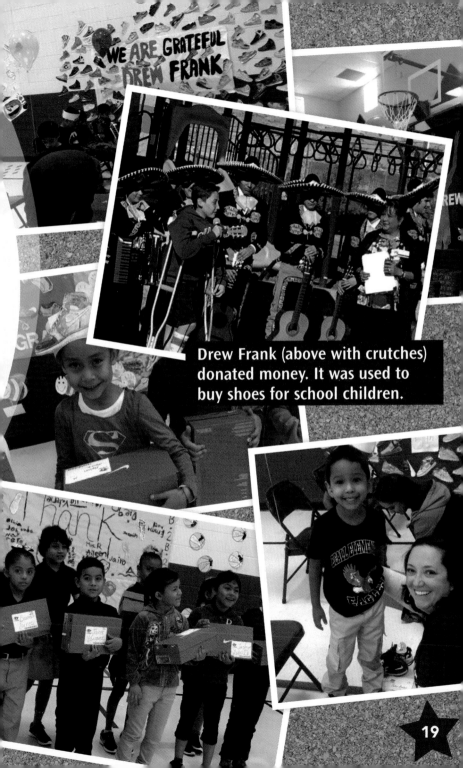

Drew Frank (above with crutches) donated money. It was used to buy shoes for school children.

If the Shoe Fits

Drew is from El Paso, Texas. He donated the money to the Braden Aboud Memorial Foundation. This group gave socks and tennis shoes to three groups. Half of the shoes went to an **orphanage** and a center for women and kids. The rest were given to students at an elementary school. All the people who received shoes live in Drew's city.

Drew said he did not need gifts. He already had a lot of toys. He just wanted to help others. And now 800 people have new shoes! Drew did not do it to get thanks. But he received thank-you signs anyway.

Drew Frank

A Good Foundation

Drew worked with the Braden Aboud Memorial Foundation. This group has helped kids in El Paso since 2007. Its goal is to help them learn and stay healthy. It raises money for shoes, blankets, and college funds.

Friend to Animals

Willow Phelps has spent many years helping people and animals. And she is only nine years old! Willow loves animals. She understands the bond between people and their pets.

Willow lives in New Jersey. She used her love of pets to help homeless people. Willow sewed cat toys. She put a tag on each toy telling about groups that help the homeless. She bought socks for those in need with money from selling her cat toys. She also bought sleeping bags and coats.

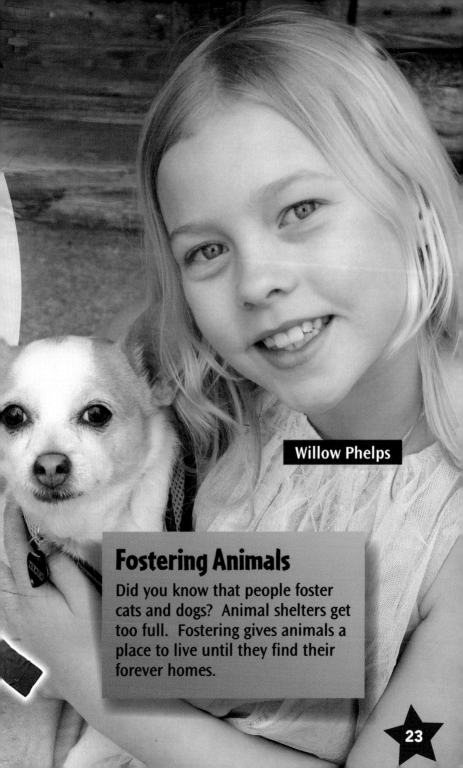

Willow Phelps

Fostering Animals

Did you know that people foster cats and dogs? Animal shelters get too full. Fostering gives animals a place to live until they find their forever homes.

23

Help Is Its Own Reward

Willow likes to help others. She does not do it to get an award. But Willow impresses many people. The ASPCA® honored her for all her hard work. In 2016, she was named the ASPCA Tommy P. Monahan Kid of the Year.

Willow works at a local shelter. One time, she swam a mile for charity to help a kitten! Willow raised funds to pay for a surgery for the cat's leg. Willow cares about all animals. She has even helped chimps and orca whales!

About Tommy P. Monahan

In 2007, Tommy was nine years old. His house caught on fire. He died trying to save his pets. The ASPCA created the Kid of the Year award in honor of Tommy and his love of animals.

It Is Your Turn

These fantastic kids have shown how easy it can be to help others. Now it is your turn. Volunteer at an animal shelter, or find ways to help the homeless. Do you have some clothes or toys you do not use anymore? Donate them. These things do not cost any money, and they make life better for someone else—whether it is a person or an animal.

You do not have to fix the whole world. Even small actions can have a big impact. A little work can change your part of the world.

Help Others and Yourself

Helping others makes you be a better person. People who give back often learn skills to become leaders and have a greater respect for others. Those skills last your whole life.

27

Glossary

access—the ability to use

charity—an organization that helps people in need and raises money for this purpose

deodorant—something people use to hide body odor

donated—gave money or items to a charity or an individual

inspired—caused someone to act

orphanage—a group home for orphans, children whose parent has died or is unable to be a parent

volunteer—to donate your time to help someone or an organization

Index

Check It Out!

Books

Boelts, Maribeth. 2009. *Those Shoes*. Candlewick.

De la Peña, Matt. 2015. *Last Stop On Market Street*. G.P. Putnam's Sons Books for Young Readers.

Pearson, Emily. 2002. *Ordinary Mary's Extraordinary Deed*. Gibbs Smith.

Websites

www.ASPCA.org

www.khloekares.com

www.freedomservicedogs.org

Try It!

You have read about kids starting charities. Now it is your turn! Create a charity or way to help others. Perhaps you want to help animals, homeless people, or kids in need.

- What will you make or sell to help others?

- How will you get the word out about your charity?

- Write a mission statement for your charity. It should be two to three sentences that explain what your charity does.

About the Author

Elizabeth Anderson Lopez lives in California with her husband and many pets. They have a parrot, a tortoise, and seven chickens! They also have a rescue dog. Lopez donates clothes and other items to charities. She also cleans up after all those pets!